W9-ANU-085

Date: 7/10/19

J 530.8 BUS
Bussiere, Desirée,
What in the world is a ton? :
and other weight & volume

SandCastle™
Let's Measure More

WHAT
IN THE
WORLD
IS A
TON?

AND OTHER
WEIGHT & VOLUME
MEASUREMENTS

A Division of ABDO
ABDO
Publishing Company

Desirée Bussiere

Consulting Editor, Diane Craig, M.A./Reading Specialist

visit us at www.abdopublishing.com

Published by ABDO Publishing Company, a division of ABDO, P.O. Box 398166, Minneapolis, Minnesota 55439. Copyright © 2013 by Abdo Consulting Group, Inc. International copyrights reserved in all countries. No part of this book may be reproduced in any form without written permission from the publisher. SandCastle™ is a trademark and logo of ABDO Publishing Company.

Printed in the United States of America, North Mankato, Minnesota
102012
012013

Editor: Liz Salzmann
Content Developer: Nancy Tuminelly
Cover and Interior Design: Colleen Dolphin, Mighty Media, Inc.
Cover and Interior Production: Kate Hartman
Photo Credits: Shutterstock

Library of Congress Cataloging-in-Publication Data

Bussierre, Desireé, 1989-
 What in the world is a ton? : and other weight & volume measurements / Desireé Bussierre ; consulting editor, Diane Craig, M.A./reading specialist.
    pages cm. -- (Let's measure more)
 Audience: 4-9
 ISBN 978-1-61783-599-5
 1. Volume--Juvenile literature. 2. Weights and measures--Juvenile literature. 3. Units of measurement--Juvenile literature. I. Title.
 QC104.B87 2013
 530.8'1--dc23
                                    2012025987

SandCastle™ Level: Transitional

SandCastle™ books are created by a team of professional educators, reading specialists, and content developers around five essential components—phonemic awareness, phonics, vocabulary, text comprehension, and fluency—to assist young readers as they develop reading skills and strategies and increase their general knowledge. All books are written, reviewed, and leveled for guided reading, early reading intervention, and Accelerated Reader® programs for use in shared, guided, and independent reading and writing activities to support a balanced approach to literacy instruction. The SandCastle™ series has four levels that correspond to early literacy development. The levels are provided to help teachers and parents select appropriate books for young readers.

Emerging Readers
(no flags)

Beginning Readers
(1 flag)

Transitional Readers
(2 flags)

Fluent Readers
(3 flags)

Contents

Weight is how heavy something is.

Volume is how much space something takes up.

weight & volume?

What is

The pound is used to measure weight. It is mostly used in the United States.

a pound?

Donny visits the doctor.
He stands on the scale.
He weighs 65 pounds.

An ounce is part of a pound.
There are 16 ounces in
1 pound.

an ounce?

Leah is at the store. She weighs an orange. The orange weighs 8 ounces.

The ton is a large unit of weight. It measures very heavy things. There are 2,000 pounds in 1 ton.

a ton?

Mike loves elephants. He sees one at the zoo. It weighs 7 tons!

The fluid ounce is used to measure liquid volume. Cans of food are measured in fluid ounces.

fluid ounce?

Alice is having soup for lunch. The can of soup is 19 ounces.

The pint is also used to measure volume. It is often used for dairy products such as milk, yogurt, and ice cream.

a pint?

Ed has ice cream on his birthday. **Chocolate** is his favorite! Ed's mom bought 2 pints.

A gallon is used to measure large volumes of liquid. There are 8 pints in a gallon. Milk and juice come in gallons.

a gallon?

Jane's dad buys 1 gallon of milk. Jane drinks milk at dinner.

A grain is a very small unit of weight. It was based on a grain of wheat.

Now it is used for **bullets** and arrows.

a grain?

Kyle has a new bow. He shoots arrows at a **target**. He uses 80-grain points on his arrows.

A carat is used to measure **gemstones. Diamonds** are measured in carats.

a carat?

Claire's mother got a new **necklace.** It has a 2-carat **diamond.**

Fun facts

⇨ Weight depends on **gravity**. There is less gravity on the moon than on Earth. So objects weigh less there.

⇨ In **ancient** Egypt, weight was measured in debens.

⇨ The Statue of Liberty weighs 225 tons.

⇨ The carat was first used in the 1400s.

⇨ There are at least 660,000 gallons of water in an Olympic-sized swimming pool.

Quiz

Read each sentence below. Then decide whether it is true or false.

1. There are 16 ounces in 1 pound. True or False?

2. Elephants can be weighed in tons. True or False?

3. A fluid ounce is used to measure liquid volume. True or False?

4. A gallon is used to measure small volumes of liquid. True or False?

5. **Diamonds** are measured in pints. True or False?

Answers: 1. True   2. True   3. True   4. False   5. False

Glossary

ancient – very long ago or very old.

bullet – a metal object that shoots out of a gun.

chocolate – flavored with a food prepared from cacao beans. Cake, ice cream, and other desserts are often flavored with chocolate.

diamond – a shiny, clear stone used to make jewelry.

gemstone – a stone used to make jewelry. Diamonds, emeralds, and rubies are gemstones.

gravity – the natural force that pulls things toward the center of Earth.

necklace – a decoration that is worn around the neck.

target – something you aim and shoot at.